STORNOWAY PRIMARY

WESTERN ISLES LIBRARIES

Readers are requested to take great care of the books while in their
possession, and to point out any defects that they may notice in them
to the Librarian.

This book is issued for a period of twenty-one days and should be
returned on or before the latest date stamped below, but an extension
of the period of loan may be granted when desired.

DATE OF RETURN	DATE OF RETURN	DATE OF RETURN

THE FACE OF THE EARTH
GRASSLANDS
JENNY VAUGHAN

Editorial planning
Jollands Editions

MACMILLAN
EDUCATION

First published 1987

Published by
MACMILLAN EDUCATION LTD
Houndmills, Basingstoke, Hampshire RG21 2XS
and London
Companies and representatives
throughout the world

Designed and produced by BLA Publishing Limited,
Swan Court, East Grinstead, Sussex, England.

Also in LONDON · HONG KONG · TAIPEI · SINGAPORE · NEW YORK

A Ling Kee Company

Illustrations by Kevin Diaper, Sallie Alane Reason
 and BLA Publishing Limited
Colour origination by Clan Studios Limited
Printed and bound in Spain by
Gráficas Estella, S. A. Navarra.

British Library Cataloguing in Publication Data

Vaughan, Jennifer
    Grasslands. — (The face of the earth)
    — (Macmillan world library)
    1. Grassland ecology — Juvenile literature
    I. Title   II. Series
    574.5'2643   GH541.5.P7

ISBN 0-333-42631-2
ISBN 0-333-42620-7 Series

Acknowledgements
The Publishers wish to thank the following organizations for their invaluable assistance in the preparation of this book.

Australian Information Service
Netherlands Board of Tourism

Photographic credits
t = top b = bottom l = left r = right

cover: ZEFA

4 The Hutchison Library; 5t ZEFA; 5b Jonathan Scott/Seaphot; 6 Douglas Dickens; 7 South American Pictures; 9t Steve Nicholls/Seaphot; 9b Douglas Dickens; 10 Jeff Foot/Survival Anglia; 11 Jen & Des Bartlett/Survival Anglia; 12 Jonathan Scott/Seaphot; 13 South American Pictures; 14 R. Knightbridge/NHPA; 14/15, 15 Richard Matthews/Seaphot; 16 Stephen Dalton/NHPA; 17t John Shaw/NHPA; 17b, 18 Jonathan Scott/Seaphot; 19t Peter Johnson/NHPA; 19b Australian Information Service; 20, 21 Jonathan Scott/Seaphot; 22 Douglas Dickins; 23t The Hutchison Library; 23b N.A. Callow/NHPA; 28 ZEFA; 29t, 29b The Hutchison Library; 30 Novosti Press Agency; 31t Walter Murray/NHPA; 31b Lord Forbes/Seaphot; 32, 33t, 33b ZEFA; 34 South American Pictures; 35, 36 The Hutchison Library; 37t Jonathan Scott/Seaphot; 37b The Hutchison Library; 38t Douglas Dickins; 38b Peter Stevenson/Seaphot; 39 Douglas Dickins; 40 ZEFA; 41t, 41b The Hutchison Library; 44 Netherlands Board of Tourism; 44/45 Hans Christian Heap/Seaphot; 45 R. Knightbridge/NHPA

Note to the reader
In this book there are some words in the text which are printed in **bold** type. This shows that the word is listed in the glossary on page 46. The glossary gives a brief explanation of words which may be new to you.

Contents

Introduction

About a quarter of the land on Earth is **grassland**. This is land where the main plants are grasses. Grasslands are often very large flat, treeless areas of land called **plains**. You can see where the grasslands are if you look at the map on page 24. The world's grasslands lie between the forests and the deserts.

On each side of the **Equator** there are grasslands called **savannas**. These types of grassland are found only in hot lands. There are also grasslands in the cooler lands to the north and south of the savannas. In Asia, they are called **steppes** and they cover a huge area.

▼ These grasslands are next to the mountains. Many different grasses and wild flowers grow here in the spring after the snow has melted.

People and grasslands

The first people had to move around the plains in order to find food. They ate berries and hunted the animals which **grazed** on the plains. Later, they tamed, or **domesticated**, sheep, goats, cattle and other animals. They kept them for meat, milk and clothing.

Then, people built homes near the forests. They did not need to travel to find food. People grew **crops** from some types of grass and began to farm the land. Wheat, rice and other food crops come from these early grasses.

Using the grasslands

The number of people in the world, the world **population**, grew every year. More people were using the land for crops and animals. They found useful **minerals** and other **natural resources**, such as salt and oil, in the grasslands. The towns grew larger as more people came to live and work on the grasslands.

◄ Grasslands are not always flat. These hills are in Afghanistan. In summer, shepherds and their herds of sheep and goats live on the hills.

Today, the population is still growing. The grasslands are too small. In some countries, people are cutting down the forest so they can grow crops. In other countries, people have used the grasslands too much. The land has turned into a desert. The land needs to be watered, or **irrigated**, to make crops grow. In the Netherlands, they have made 'new' land. The Dutch have drained, or **reclaimed**, the land from the sea to make grassland.

Looking after the grasslands

Wild animals used to move freely on the grasslands. Then, people killed many of the animals. People used the land to grow crops or to build homes. Not much grassland was left for the wild animals. Some types, or **species**, of animal have almost disappeared. In North America, there are special parks for the bison. In Africa, there are special parks for elephants, lions and other animals.

The grasslands themselves are also in danger. In some areas, people have not looked after the grasslands. The grass has died and the soil has blown away. These areas become deserts. People also use **chemicals** to help crops grow. These chemicals often kill plants and insects on the grasslands. Now, people are trying to protect the grasslands. This is called **conservation**.

◄ People are not allowed to kill this Cape Buffalo. It lives in the Masai Mara Game Park in Kenya.

Making grasslands

Some grasslands are millions of years old. Other grasslands are newer. On the old grasslands, grass grows well but trees find it hard to grow. There is not enough rain and sometimes the soil is wrong or too shallow for the trees. These are called **natural** grasslands. The new grasslands were made by people. They cut down the forests to make land to grow crops. They also made **pastures** where their animals could feed on good grass. These are called **cultivated** grasslands.

Grasslands long ago

Millions of years ago, there were forests on the plains of North America. Then, mountains, like the Rockies, were made on the west side of the **continent**. The new mountains changed the weather, or **climate**. More rain fell on the land between the sea and the mountains. The plains on

▲ This forest in Sri Lanka is being cut down and burned. New grasslands are being made. The land will be ploughed and crops will be planted.

the other side became much drier. They were in the **rain shadow** of the mountains. In summer, there was often no rain at all. This is called **drought**. The forests died and grass grew instead. Grasslands also appeared in other parts of the world, like the steppes of the USSR and China.

Clouds carrying rain blow from the sea toward a range of mountains. The rain falls on the side of the mountains nearest the sea. The wind blows over the mountains. By the time the wind reaches the other side of the mountains, most of the rain has fallen and the clouds have gone. This means that one side of the mountain is much drier than the other. We say the drier side is in the rain shadow.

► This herd of llamas is grazing on the altiplano in Bolivia in South America. The altiplano is a grassy plain above the tree line in the Andes Mountains.

Fire and animals

When the grasslands have been made, fire and animals help to stop other plants growing. Grasslands can catch fire when lightning hits the ground during a storm. The hot sun can also start a fire if the grass is very dry. Fire kills trees or other plants which are starting to grow. The tough grass survives. After the fire, the grass grows thicker and stronger.

People often burn the grass to give their animals better pasture. Animals prefer the young green grass which grows after a fire. Animals also eat the new shoots of plants and trees so they cannot grow.

The high grasslands

There are grasslands high up in the mountains. Trees cannot grow because the climate is cold and dry. The soil is thin and poor. These areas are above the **tree line**. The tree line is the height above which trees will not grow.

In some places, like the Andes Mountains of South America, there are huge rolling plains above the tree line. In other high places, like the Alps of Europe and the Himalayas of Asia, there are small, grassy **meadows**. Many types of grass and flowers can grow there. They can survive the winter snows.

7

Grassland plants

Grasses have slim, hollow stems and straight, narrow leaves. There are about 8000 types of grass. Many types of grass often grow in the same place. Many grasses are only a few centimetres high. Others can grow as high as 4m.

Grasses and climate

Grasses are well **adapted** to hard conditions. Many can live, or **survive**, through drought and floods. These can kill other types of plant. Some kinds of grass can survive when it is very hot or very cold.

Grasses can grow very fast. Some kinds shoot up, produce seeds and die in a very short time. These are **annual** grasses. They are the first plants to grow at the edge of desert areas after rain. Annual grasses produce many seeds. Some seeds fall from the plant and lie in the soil below. Other seeds are blown a long way by the wind. The seeds are tough. Many survive until the next rains come. Then, they become new plants.

Annual grasses rot when they die. This adds goodness to the soil. The soil becomes more **fertile**. Other types of grass can start to grow then. These are **perennial** grasses. They go on growing year after year. Perennial grasses produce seeds. They also spread by sending long stems along or under the ground. New plants grow from these stems. The soil is soon full of roots. The roots help to hold any water in the soil. They stop the rain from washing the soil away.

Perennial grasses grow thicker and stronger each time they are eaten by animals. New shoots grow again quickly. The droppings from the animals also help to make the soil richer.

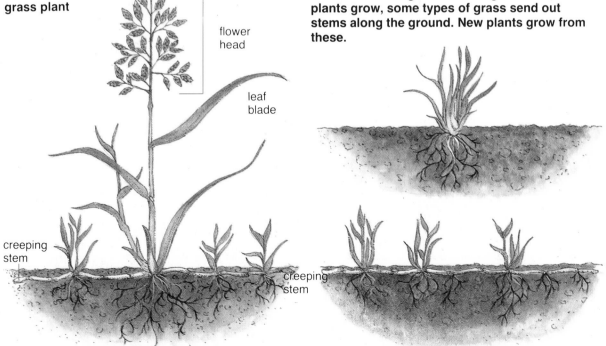

A typical grass plant

flower head

leaf blade

creeping stem

creeping stem

roots

▼ Grass seedlings start as single tufts. As the plants grow, some types of grass send out stems along the ground. New plants grow from these.

Many types of plant

Grasses are not the only grassland plants. Natural grasslands often have many kinds of flowers as well. Wild tulips and lilies grow on the steppes of Asia. Poppies cover the ground on some grasslands in North America. Some small trees and **shrubs**, like the **acacia** (*a-kay-sha*), can grow in dry places. Acacias grow on the grasslands of Africa, South America and Australia.

Grassland farmers grow crops which they can sell. They often choose grasses called **cereals**. These have large seeds, or **grain**. People and animals eat grain. Cereals include wheat, maize, barley and rice. The plants are strong and grow fast.

▲ This British meadow is hundreds of years old. It is natural grassland. The purple flowers are fritillaries. They are very rare flowers. The meadow is protected by law so people and animals do not destroy it.

▶ These people are harvesting rice in southern Asia. Rice is a type of grass. It is a very important cereal crop. It is grown to feed millions of people in the hot countries of the world.

9

Cool grasslands

Grasslands in cool climates are called **temperate** grasslands. They are often in the centre of continents. In winter, it is very cold and strong winds blow. The grass is covered with snow. In spring, new green shoots appear. There is about 25 to 75 cm of rain a year. Most of the rain falls in spring and early summer. The summers are very hot. The grass turns yellow.

From forest to desert

A temperate grassland does not have the same climate everywhere. When it is next to a forest, there is more rain. The soil is more fertile and the grass can grow up to 3 m high. Near a desert, there is less rain. The soil is poor and the grass is shorter. The wetter grasslands are sometimes called **prairies**. The drier grasslands are sometimes called steppes.

Grasslands of the north

There are two very large areas of grasslands between the Equator and the North Pole. In North America, the eastern

Grasslands are found between the world's forests and deserts. All plants need water to make them grow. Grass grows taller on the grasslands near the wet forests and shorter near the dry deserts.

▲ These bison are grazing on the dry shortgrass prairies of North America

Desert

Shortgrass prairies or steppes

Very poor soil
Drought

Poor soil
Low rainfall

part of the grasslands is next to the forests. It is the wettest part. It is called tallgrass prairie. Further west, the grasses get shorter. There is less rain. The shortgrass prairies are next to the Rocky Mountains. They are almost desert. Farmers grow wheat on the tallgrass and midgrass prairies. They keep cattle on the shortgrass areas.

The steppes of Central Europe and Asia lie between the wet forests in the north and the deserts in the south. Farmers may plant this land with a type of grass called **alfalfa**, or **lucerne**, for cattle and sheep to eat. Alfalfa looks like clover.

Grasslands of the south

There are some large grassland areas in the southern half of the world. One of the best known areas is the **pampas** in South America. Pampa is the word for a plain. The pampas cover a large part of Argentina, Brazil and Uruguay. Near the east coast, the pampas have a wetter climate. It gets drier and the grass is shorter further inland.

The cool grasslands in southern Africa are called the **veld**. The Australian cool grasslands are often called **downs**. Farmers grow cereals, such as wheat, in these areas. They also keep large flocks of sheep.

Forest

Tallgrass and midgrass prairies

Good soil
Medium rainfall

Rich, deep soil
High rainfall

▲ Springtime on the veld in southern Africa. The zebra are feeding on the young shoots which have grown after the rain.

Hot grasslands

Countries near the Equator have a hot or **tropical** climate. The tropics are the hot, damp areas on either side of the Equator. The climate is hot all year round. It rains once or twice a year. In grassland areas, there may be more than 100 cm of rain each year. When it rains, green grass grows very quickly. Then, there is drought. The grass dries up and turns brown in the drought.

Savanna grasslands

Savanna grasslands are mainly grass with a few trees. They look like large parks. They lie between the tropical forests and the deserts. The forests are very wet. They are **rain forests**. The savanna next to the forests has tall thick grasses. Close to the desert, the grasses are short and thin. There are many types of grass on savanna grasslands.

The trees of the savanna have deep strong roots. They can reach the water underground. Some trees have roots that spread out far from the tree. These can collect moisture from a large area. Acacia trees lose their leaves when it is dry. This helps to stop the trees from losing moisture. The trees grow taller near the wet forests. There are more trees near the forests. Trees, shrubs and grasses also grow near water holes and along river beds, where there is more water.

There are many kinds of animal on the savanna. This is because the places, or **habitats**, for the animals to live are so varied on the savanna.

▼ You can see how dry it gets on the African savanna. These trees are acacias. The elephants eat the bark and leaves.

▲ These grasslands are part of the llanos in Venezuela. A river has flooded on to the llanos. Most of the time it is dry and hot. When the rains come and the rivers flood, new green plants grow.

Africa and South America

The world's largest savannas are in Africa. They surround the tropical forests in the centre of the continent. The Sahara Desert lies to the north of the savanna. The Kalahari Desert lies to the south west. It is hard to grow crops to feed people and animals near the desert. The people sometimes keep cattle and goats. Closer to the Equator, the climate is wetter. The people can grow crops.

South America also has large areas of savanna. In the north, in Venezuela, it is called **llanos**. Further south, it is called **campos**. The winters are warm and the summers are very hot. Most of the rain falls in the summer in heavy thunderstorms. The grasses and other plants are often very dry and brown. After the rain, the new shoots turn the campos green.

Australia and India

In Australia, the grasslands lie between huge areas of desert and tropical forests. They have less rain than the savanna of Africa. It is often very hot and windy. Farmers keep sheep and cattle. Many kinds of eucalyptus (*you-ca-lip-tus*) tree grow there.

People have made tropical grasslands in India. They cut down the trees and cleared the land. In very dry areas, they had to irrigate the soil. Now the farmers can grow cereals and other crops.

Insects and birds

The world's grasslands have many types of plants, animals, insects and birds. They depend on each other in order to survive. In the African savanna, plant-eating animals eat the grasses. The meat-eaters eat the plant-eaters. Some birds eat the remains of the dead animals. This is called a **food chain**.

Insects

Insects are an important part of the grassland food chain. They feed on plants and other living things. They provide food for other insects, birds and animals. Some insects, like the dung beetle, help to make the soil richer. In Africa, the dung beetles bury the animal droppings. This makes the soil more fertile.

Termites live in the grasslands of Africa and South America. They chew up wood and other plants to make their huge nests. Anteaters and armadillos eat the termites.

Many kinds of grasshopper live in the grasslands. The locust is a kind of grasshopper. Locusts can harm the grasslands. They sometimes move in large **swarms**. There may be more than 1000 million insects in a swarm. They travel across the grasslands and eat the crops. A large swarm can eat up to 3000 tonnes of green plants in one day.

Some insects carry diseases. The tsetse (*tet-see*) fly carries sleeping sickness which is a dangerous disease in Africa. The female feeds on animal and human blood.

▶ The Adonis blue butterfly is found in Europe. These butterflies are in danger. Farmers kill the plants they eat. When their food is gone, the butterflies cannot survive.

▲ This is part of the South American pampas. It is flat and grassy. The animals are pampas deer. The brown mounds are termite nests. There can be more than a million termites in a nest. A termite queen can lay up to 30 000 eggs a day, for 20 years.

Birds

Birds are also an important part of the grassland food chain. A grasshopper eats a plant. A small bird eats the grasshopper. A large **bird of prey**, like an owl, or an animal eats the small bird.

Sometimes, people break the food chain and wild animals die. When grasslands are burned, there are no seeds or insects for the birds. Farmers use chemicals to kill insects. Birds eat the poisoned insects. They may die too.

There are many kinds of bird on the grasslands. They may have to fly a long way looking for food and water. There are few trees to nest in. Many, like the lark, nest in the grass. Others, like the prairie chicken, lay their eggs on the ground. In the savanna, weaver birds hang their nests from the branches of shrubs and trees.

Many brightly coloured birds live near water holes in the Australian savanna. There are green budgerigars and bright blue mulga parrots.

The world's largest bird is the ostrich. It lives in the African grasslands. It is about 2.5 m tall. It cannot fly, but it can run at a speed of about 60 kph. The South American rhea and the Australian emu are both grassland birds. They are like the ostrich, but smaller.

The bustard is another large grassland bird. The largest bustard is the African kori. It can be up to 1.5 m tall. The Australian bustard is almost as big.

▼ The skylark is a grassland bird. It makes its nest on the ground in the tall grass. The colour of the skylark helps it to hide in the grass.

Plant-eating animals

Many grassland animals eat only grass. They are the plant-eaters. Animals which hunt other animals for meat are called **predators**. They eat the plant-eaters. Many plant-eating animals live on the grasslands.

The burrowers

Some grassland animals are **rodents**. These are small animals with long, sharp front teeth which they use for gnawing.

Rodents are well adapted to grassland life. They can eat every part of a plant. They eat the roots, seeds and leaves. They often live in **burrows**. Inside, they are safe from predators. The burrows also protect the rodents from the hot sun.

There are many burrowers in the South American pampas. These include the cavy, a wild guinea pig, the long-legged mara and the tuco-tuco. The tuco-tuco gets its name from the noise it makes. The prairie dog of North America also burrows under the ground. The burrows join up to make 'cities'. One prairie dog city covered more than 40 000 sq km. Millions of prairie dogs lived there.

◄ The harvest mouse is a rodent. It lives in Europe among the cereal crops grown by farmers. It feeds on seeds and grain like the grains of wheat in this picture. In the summer, the harvest mouse builds a nest attached to the stems of crops and long grass. Rodents like these are food for many predators like owls and foxes.

▲ The prairie dog is not a dog at all. It is a rodent living on the prairies of North America. Its call sounds like a dog barking. This prairie dog is on guard and watching for danger.

▼ Impala are a type of antelope. They graze on the grasslands of Africa. The impala can jump a length of more than nine metres to escape from predators.

Grazers and browsers

Grazers are animals which eat grass. **Browsers** are animals which go from plant to plant, eating leaves and twigs.

Many kinds of plant-eating animals live on the African savanna. Tall giraffes browse on the leaves at the top of trees. Elephants eat the leaves, twigs and **bark**. The black rhino browses on the lower branches. Zebras and antelopes are grazers. They live in large herds. This helps to protect them from predators. They can also run fast from danger.

There are plant-eaters in other grassland areas, too. Wallabies and kangaroos live on the Australian grasslands. Pampas deer live in South America. The wild ass and wild horse live on the Central Asian steppes.

People nearly destroyed many of the grassland plant-eaters. Very large numbers of bison and pronghorn antelopes used to live on the American prairies. Many of the animals were hunted and killed. The saiga deer used to live on the Asian steppes. Now, laws have been made which stop people from killing the animals.

Cattle, sheep and other domestic animals live on temperate grassland farms. These animals are usually grazers or browsers.

Meat-eating animals

Many kinds of meat-eating animals live on the grasslands. The predators hunt and eat other animals. There are two main families of predators. These are the cats and the dogs. **Scavengers** are animals which feed on the remains of food left by the predators.

The big cats

Lions, leopards and cheetahs all belong to the cat family. They are large, strong animals. They are found mainly in the grasslands of Africa.

Lions are the only members of the cat family that hunt in groups. The lionesses do most of the work. They surround a herd of antelopes or zebras. They pick out and attack the weakest animals.

The cheetah stalks, or creeps up on its prey. This is often an antelope or a gazelle. The cheetah gets close to its prey, and then leaps out at it. The cheetah can run very fast over a short distance. It can reach speeds of more than 90 kph.

The cheetah and the lion are both **camouflaged**. This means their colour makes it hard for other animals to see them. Lions and cheetahs have yellow-brown coats which are the same colour as the grass on the savanna. The cheetah's spots also help it to hide in the grass.

The leopard also lives on the savanna. It has darker spots than the cheetah. The leopard is related to the jaguar. The jaguar and the puma are found on the grasslands of North and South America.

▼ This lioness has sprung out of hiding to attack a group of zebras. After the kill, the lioness may feed her cubs, or the lion may eat first.

▼ The leopard is very well camouflaged. Its spots make it hard for other animals to see it among the bushes of the African savanna.

Packs of dogs

Wild dogs are smaller than the big cats. They often hunt in packs. They chase their **prey** until it is tired out.

Packs of wild dogs roam the African savanna. The wild dogs of Australia are called dingoes. The coyotes or wild dogs of North America are related to wolves. There are wolves on the steppes of Asia and Europe.

Scavengers

Scavengers eat the dead meat left by predators. Vultures, jackals and hyenas are scavengers. The jackals and hyenas watch the vultures. They see where the birds find food and follow them. The jackals and hyenas have strong teeth and jaws to crack the bones.

Jackals and hyenas are hunters as well as scavengers. When these large animals have finished eating, smaller animals take over. Crows, rats and ants finish the meat of dead animals left by predators.

▼ The dingo is a wild dog which lives only in Australia. It is a meat-eater and feeds on kangaroos, sheep and chickens.

On the move

Some grassland animals travel long distances. They move from place to place to find food. They like to eat young, fresh grass. They move in large herds. This is called **migration**.

Searching for food

Animals migrate for a number of reasons. When the **seasons** change, the weather changes. If the weather is cold, some animals move to warmer places. When the grass dries up after the rainy season the animals also move to fresh grasslands.

In the African savanna, large herds of wildebeeste still travel across the Serengeti National Park, in Tanzania. In May, they are in the south east of the park. The weather is very dry. The wildebeeste move north east to wetter places. Many zebras travel with them. They reach Kenya in June and July. The grass is still green there. The animals stay in Kenya until November. Then, there is rain in the south again. The animals travel south and the females have their calves. The whole journey covers about 500 km.

The females have their calves during the rainy season. There is plenty of food for them to eat.

▼ The animals in this picture are wildebeeste. They have heavy bodies and long thin legs. They have big heads with horns.

▲ These Masai herders live with their cattle on the savanna of Kenya and Tanzania.

People and animals

Some grassland people who keep animals do not stay in one place. They move to find good grass for their animals. When that has been eaten, they move on again. People who live like this are called **pastoral nomads**.

Several groups of nomads live in the African savanna. These include the Masai. They often keep large herds of cattle. The Masai also keep some sheep, goats and donkeys.

The Masai **herders** live near rivers or wells. Their cattle eat the grass nearby. The Masai move on when the grass gets dry and the water dries up. When they **settle** in a new place, they build houses from twigs, mud and cattle dung. They build a fence around the houses. They keep their animals inside the fences at night. This is to keep them safe from animals like leopards and lions.

The Masai used to live off the food they produced from their cattle. Now the Masai can buy food. They cannot travel as far as they used to. Much of their old land has been turned into cattle farms, or **ranches**. Some of these are owned by Masai people. A few Masai grow crops now instead of keeping cattle. Some have jobs in towns.

There are fewer nomads on the world's grasslands than there used to be. Groups of nomads live on the steppes of Asia. In many other places, the grasslands have been fenced in. There is no longer the space for many people to live on the move.

Early farmers

Thousands of years ago, people were hunters. Then, they found that some grasses were good to eat. They learned to plant seeds and grow their own food.

People settled in one place. The first farmers cleared a patch of grassland or forest. They grew crops there for a few years. They moved on when the soil was worn out. Some of the first farmers lived in the Middle East. We know that people grew crops 10 000 years ago in Mesopotamia. The area is now called Iran and Iraq.

New ways of farming

People began to learn better ways of using the land to grow crops. They were able to farm in one place year after year. In Egypt, they found that crops grew well along the River Nile. The Nile flooded every year and spread water and soil over the land. The soil it left behind was very fertile. The farmers also learned that crops grew better if they dug up and turned the soil. People used sharp stones or sticks to dig. Then the Egyptians **invented** the plough. People or animals could pull the plough along the ground to turn the soil.

The Egyptians made simple **machines** to lift the water from the river. They used this water to irrigate their crops.

Farmers learned to use animal dung to make the soil richer. They learned to remove weeds. They also found that crops grew best if they grew different crops in turn on the same land.

▼ These women live in the country of Ecuador in South America. They are planting potatoes. Most of their work in the fields is done by hand. Their way of life has not changed much for hundreds of years.

The farmers

Ways of farming, or **agriculture**, stayed the same for hundreds of years. Today, some farmers still use animals to pull ploughs and carts. They still cut their crops by hand. These farmers have small farms. They grow food for themselves and their families. This kind of farming is called **subsistence** farming.

In many countries, people now have machines to help them farm. Farmers use tractors for many of the jobs that animals once did. Tractors pull ploughs and machines for planting and weeding. Farmers also use **combine harvesters**. These are large machines that do all the work of **harvesting**. They cut the crops. Then, they separate the straw or stalks and put the grain into bags.

Machines made farming the land easier and quicker. Farmers could grow more crops. They could sell the crops. Now, large areas of the temperate grasslands are sown with crops to sell, or **cash crops**.

▲ It is harvest time in this village near Beijing in China. The people are cutting the crops by hand.

▼ These farmers in Austria are making hay. The cut grass is hanging in the sun to dry. When it is dry, the hay will be stored and then fed to their animals.

Grasslands of the world

The world's grasslands are very large open spaces. They lie between the forests and the deserts. There are few trees because there is not enough rain. Some grasslands have only grass. Other grasslands have grass and other plants, as well as trees and shrubs.

People and grasslands

In many places, people have changed the grasslands. They want to grow food for people and their animals. Sometimes, people make new grasslands. They cut down the forests or water the desert lands.

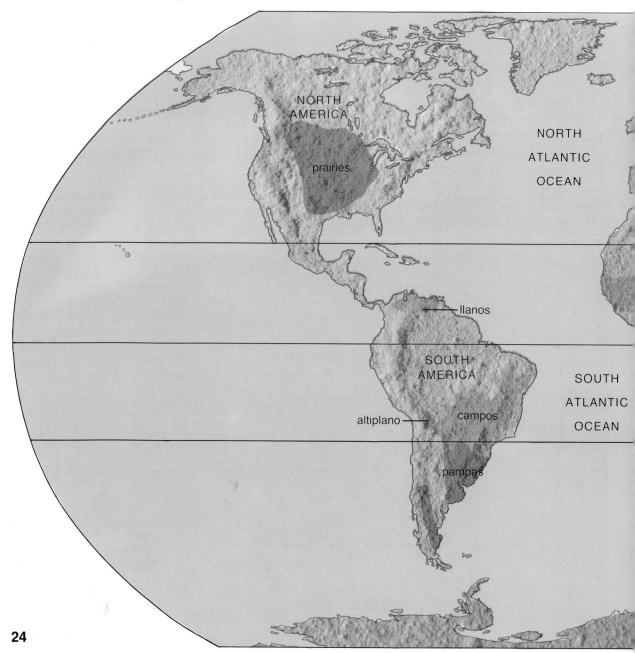

Most of the cool grasslands are used by farmers. In wet areas, there are very large fields of wheat and maize. One wheat field in the Canadian prairies covered over 14 000 hectares. There are very large buildings called silos which are used to store the grain in after the harvests. The largest silo is in Texas. It can hold more than 700 million litres of grain.

Farmers keep animals in the drier parts of cool grasslands. In Mongolia, in Central Asia, there are just over a million people. There are more than 20 million sheep, goats, cattle, horses and camels on the steppes of Mongolia.

Crops are harder to grow in the hot grasslands. If there is a drought, all the crops may die. Most farmers there keep animals. One person is said to have owned 250 000 cattle in Brazil's campos.

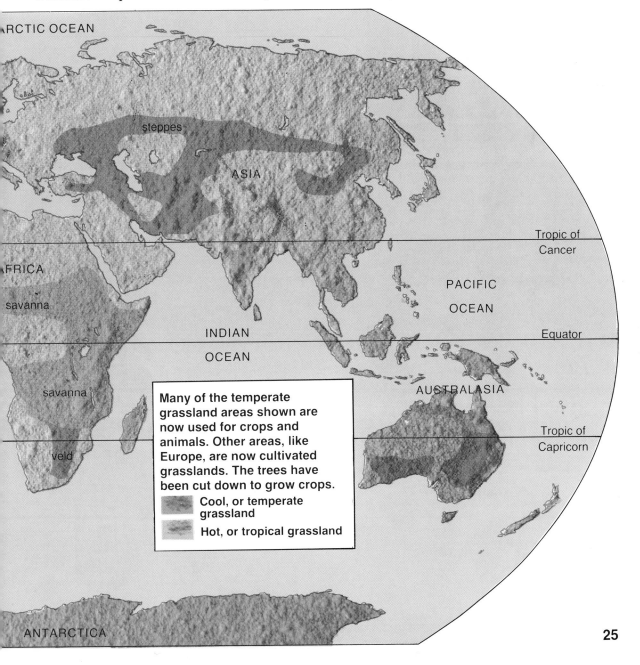

ARCTIC OCEAN

steppes

ASIA

Tropic of Cancer

AFRICA

savanna

PACIFIC OCEAN

INDIAN OCEAN

Equator

savanna

AUSTRALASIA

veld

Tropic of Capricorn

Many of the temperate grassland areas shown are now used for crops and animals. Other areas, like Europe, are now cultivated grasslands. The trees have been cut down to grow crops.

Cool, or temperate grassland

Hot, or tropical grassland

ANTARCTICA

Food for the world

Cereals are the world's most important food. People eat cereals, such as rice, barley and oats. They also eat food made from the cereals, such as bread, porridge and biscuits. Domestic animals also eat cereals. The animals produce milk, meat and eggs. Cereals are grown on nearly three quarters of the land where people grow food. Over half of these cereals are wheat, rice and corn.

Wheat, rice and corn

Wheat has been grown for over 4000 years. It is the world's most important crop. People grow more than 500 million tonnes each year. Wheat grows best on the

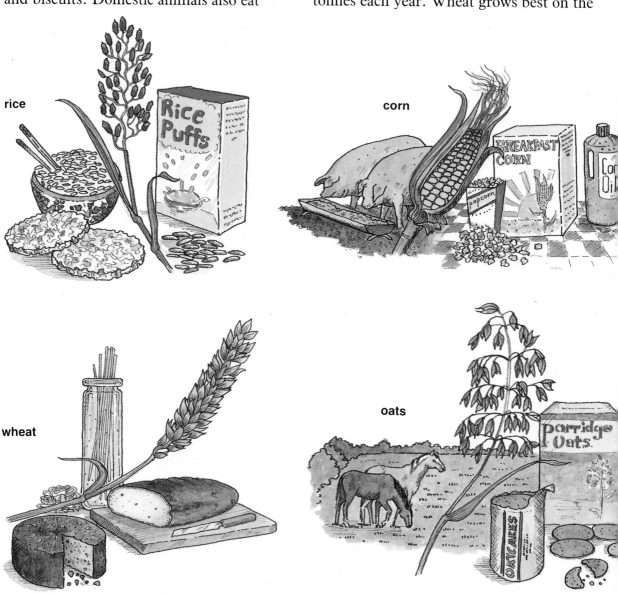

rice

corn

wheat

oats

cool grasslands in Argentina, Australia, Canada, the United States and the USSR. Wheat grows well when there is a cool, wet spring and a warm dry summer. People eat wheat grains and other foods made from wheat. They use wheat flour for bread, cakes and pies. Another kind of wheat, called durum wheat, grows in drier areas. This is used for making pasta.

Rice is the world's second most important crop. About 450 million tonnes are grown each year. Rice is the main, or **staple**, food for millions of people in parts of India, China and South East Asia. It grows best on the hot grasslands in India and China. Rice needs plenty of water. Farmers grow rice in areas where there is plenty of rain.

Half of the world's corn grows in North America. It also grows in China, South America and the USSR. There are many kinds of corn. People eat sweetcorn, popcorn and cornmeal. Other kinds of corn are grown to feed animals.

Other kinds of cereal

Barley is the world's third most important cereal. Barley grows on hot and cool grasslands. It is fed mainly to animals.

Millet grows on the drier grasslands in Africa, Asia and North and South America. It can survive poor soil and drought. In parts of India and Africa, millet seeds are ground and made into porridge or bread. Millet is also grown to feed animals.

Rye is grown in northern and eastern Europe and some parts of the USSR. It grows well in colder climates and poor soil. Rye flour is used to make a dark brown bread. Rye is also used to feed cattle and pigs.

Oats grow best on the damper parts of the temperate grasslands. Oat grains are often ground or chopped to make porridge and biscuits.

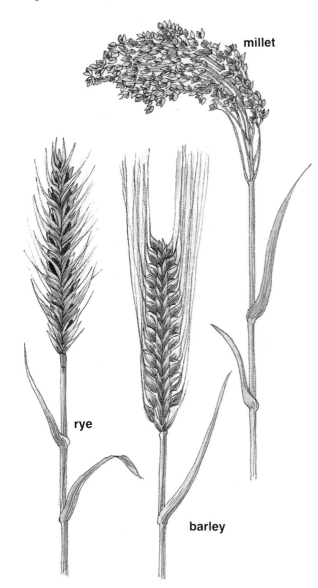

millet

rye

barley

◄ These are the world's main cereals. They give us grain which is made into food for people and animals. There are many types of plant in each group of cereals. Scientists are able to make new plants to suit different climates, or to produce more grain. Chemicals can also be added to the land in order to make it more fertile and to protect the crops from disease. These new plants and chemicals have helped farmers to double the world grain harvest in the last 25 years.

The steppes of Asia

Very large areas of grassland stretch across Central Asia. They are called the Eurasian steppes because they start in eastern Europe. Then they stretch east for about 4000 km across the USSR. They end at the Altai Mountains in Siberia. There are smaller areas of steppe land in northern China and Mongolia.

The climate changes from north to south. In the north, the steppes are next to forests. The soil is rich and trees can grow. Grass covers the central part of the steppes. The southern steppes are next to the Asian desert. The climate is drier. Most of the soil is sandy and only a few plants can grow.

A grassy highway

In the past, the steppes were used as a wide grassy road or highway. People and animals were able to travel east or west. There were no mountains, rivers or thick forests to stop them. Many groups of people travelled across the steppes from the USSR, Mongolia and China. They were looking for new land to win, or **conquer**, for themselves.

About 800 years ago, the leader of the Mongol tribe was Genghis Khan. His soldiers were fierce horsemen. The Mongols crossed the steppes to conquer much of what is now the USSR and parts of Europe. The Mongol kingdom, or **empire**, was very large.

The steppes were useful for trade. The traders travelled across the steppes in groups called **caravans**. They came from China to sell spices, cloth and other goods in Europe.

◀ The animals in this picture are two-humped Bactrian camels. They are grazing on the Mongolian steppes in Asia. In the distance, you can see the home of a group of wandering herders. The home is a kind of tent called a yurt. It is made from animal skins. When the herders move to new pastures, they take down the yurt. The camels carry the yurt and the herders' other belongings from place to place.

Life on the steppes

Many nomads used to live on the steppes. They kept herds of animals for food. The Mongols and the Kazakhs were both nomadic peoples. The Kazakhs come from Kazakhstan in the USSR. Some Kazakhs still keep sheep, goats and cattle. They need their animals for food, clothing and shelter. Kazakhs ride horses very well.

Many nomads have now become farmers. They grow cereals to sell. They keep animals on pasture lands. The very large flat wheat lands of Kazakhstan provide a lot of grain for the USSR.

In some areas, like Kazakhstan, coal, oil and minerals have been found. Roads and railways have been built across the steppes to carry these goods to other places. Many towns in the south, like Samarkand, were famous in the past. The people were skilled in making beautiful objects. People in these towns were very rich. They used to trade with other countries. Today, the people still produce cotton and silk. They make beautiful cloths and carpets. They often use old, or **traditional**, designs.

▲ These yak herders live in a region of China called the Tibetan Plateau. This is a huge, dry plain more than 4000 m above sea level. The yak is a wild ox with a shaggy coat. Yaks can survive on the poor grass in this area.

▼ Many flocks of sheep and goats graze on the dry pastures of the Chinese steppes. These Mongolian children are wearing the traditional clothes of the steppes. Their clothes keep them warm in the cold climate.

Grasslands of Europe

The steppes of the USSR stretch west from Asia into eastern Europe. The grasslands in western Europe are often cultivated grasslands. People cut down the forests to grow crops.

Eastern Europe

The grasslands of eastern Europe are very fertile. The Ukraine in the USSR is a good farming area. It also has a lot of **industry**. There are coalfields and iron **ore** mines. People there make a lot of machines and other goods in the **factories**. Nearly one fifth of the people of the USSR live there.

The soil in the Ukraine is very fertile. There are large cereal farms where they grow wheat. Crops from this area are used to feed people all over the USSR.

There are two main kinds of farm in the USSR. There are **state** farms and **collective** farms. The **government** owns the state farms. They are often very large. The workers are paid wages. Collective farms are run by groups of people. They sell their crops and divide the money between themselves.

Workers on collective farms have their own small gardens. They grow vegetables for themselves and to sell in the towns.

◀ It is harvest time on a state farm in the Ukraine. You can see how large the fields are. Many combine harvesters are needed to harvest the crop. The Ukraine is one of the most important farming areas of the USSR. There are many large state farms. Wheat, rye, sugar beet, sunflowers and vegetables all grow there. There are also cattle farms. These produce meat and milk.

30

Western Europe

Western Europe used to be mostly forest land. Now people have cut down many of the forests. They have made open fields. The farms in western Europe are often smaller than the farms on the steppes or on the prairies of North America.

The soil in western Europe is very fertile. The climate is cool and wet for much of the year. Farmers grow large amounts of cash crops, such as wheat, barley, oats and rye. They also grow fruit and vegetables to sell in the local markets and to sell to other countries.

The most important animals are dairy cattle. These are cows kept for their milk. The climate suits dairy cattle well. Britain, France, West Germany and the Netherlands produce large amounts of milk and milk products. They sell butter, cheese and some milk to other countries.

Farmers in Europe use machines to get more and better crops from their land. The machines can plough the land, sow the seed and harvest the crops. They are also used to spread fertilizer on the soil to make it richer.

▲ This farmland in England was once forest. Now, there are many fields. Farmers grow crops in some fields and raise animals in others. This is called mixed farming.

▼ These people are looking after sheep on the side of a mountain in Yugoslavia. There are large areas of natural grassland in the mountains of Europe.

The prairies of North America

▼ The prairies of North America have some of the largest farms in the world. This farmland is in the state of Kansas, United States. All you can see are the wheatfields. There are very few houses. The roads are straight for great distances.

▼ The prairies of North America have some of the largest farms in the world. This farmland is in the state of Kansas, United States. All you can see are the wheatfields. There are very few houses. The roads are straight for great distances.

The prairie grasslands are in the centre and west of the United States. They also stretch up into Canada. Forests lie to the north and east of the prairies. In the west, the prairies are called the Great Plains. They are next to the Rocky Mountains. The prairies stretch down to the desert-like land of New Mexico and Texas in the south.

The plains were once natural grassland. The Plains Indians hunted the bison which roamed the open plains. The Indians hunted on foot. Later, they used horses. The Indians followed the bison when they moved to new pastures. They ate the bison meat. They used the skins to make tents and clothes.

Ranchers and farmers

The first Europeans came to the plains in the 1700s. At first, they traded with the Indians. In the late 1800s, the new railways brought thousands of settlers to the plains. The settlers drove the Indians away. The settlers killed the bison. They fenced in the open plains to grow crops or keep cattle.

Today, there is little natural grassland on the plains. Farmers keep cattle on the shortgrass prairies in the south and west. They used to travel around the large cattle farms, or ranches, on horses. Now, they drive trucks or cars. They still use horses to round up the cattle.

Farmers grow wheat and maize on the tallgrass prairies in the north and east. Farmers use machines, like combine harvesters, to harvest the crops. Today, very few people are needed to work on the land.

The prairie farms are important for the United States and Canada. They provide food to eat and sell.

Oil

The plains also have oil. Oil is found deep under the ground. It is pumped to the surface. The oil is then pumped along pipes to a **refinery**. There, the oil is made into other products, like **fuel** to drive cars and aeroplanes. Much of America's oil comes from the plains.

There are other industries on the plains. These include making aeroplanes and farm machines, and processing the food grown in the prairies. Large cities have grown as industries have become more important on the plains.

▼ These huge buildings are called grain silos. Grain is stored in them after the harvest. There is a railway line next to the silos. Grain can be loaded on to the trains and taken quickly to the cities and ports.

▲ The machine in this picture is called a 'donkey'. It is used to pump oil to the surface from under the ground.

Grasslands of South America

The llanos and the campos are the two areas of tropical grassland in South America.

The llanos grasslands are in Venezuela. Llanos means plain. The area is low and flat. The Orinoco River flows through it. The river often floods.

The campos are in Brazil and Paraguay. They are much larger grasslands. Rivers flow into the campos. Forests grow along the river valleys. The campos grasslands have hot, dry summers. When the rains come, there may be floods.

The Mato Grosso **plateau** is part of the campos in Brazil. A plateau is an area of high flat land. The Mato Grosso is one of the wildest areas in the world. There are very large cattle ranches here. Ranchers often do not know how much land or how many cattle they have.

▼ This gaucho is riding across the pampas in Argentina. You can see that the plain is flat and treeless.

▲ These cattle have been grazing on the llanos of Venezuela. The gauchos are now rounding up the cattle that are ready for the market.

The pampas

The pampas in South America are temperate grasslands. They are in the south of the continent.

The pampas cover a large area of land in Argentina, Brazil and Uruguay. The almost flat land stretches from the Andes Mountains in the west to the Atlantic Ocean in the east.

The pampas soil is some of the richest in the world. Long ago, a tall feathery grass called pampas grass was the main plant there. Today, much of this grassland area is used for sheep and cattle farms. Farmers have planted alfalfa to feed to their cattle.

About half the area is used for crops, like wheat and corn. The other half is used for grazing land. This is furthest from the Atlantic in the west. The climate is dry there. People have to sink deep wells to get water for themselves and their animals. They use windmills to pump the water to the surface.

The pampas are very important to Argentina, Brazil and Uruguay. People make money from the pampas animals. They sell the wool, skins and beef abroad as **exports**.

South American cowboys

In the past, farmers needed cowboys to look after the cattle. South American cowboys are called gauchos (*gow-chos*). They are very good horsemen. They used to round up the cattle from the open plains. They drove them from the ranch to the market by herding them across the grasslands. Today, farmers fence their cattle in. The cattle are taken to the market by trucks. There are still some gauchos working on the farms.

Grasslands of Africa

Look at the map on page 24. You can see that much of Africa is grassland. There are several types of grassland in Africa. There are cool grasslands. There are mountain grasslands in places too high for trees to grow. There are also the hot savanna grasslands. Most of the grasslands in Africa are savanna.

Life on the savanna

There are many ways of life on the savanna. In the driest areas, people cannot grow many crops. They often live as nomads and keep cattle. In wetter areas, they may be able to settle in one place. Then, they grow crops as well as keeping cattle. The work in the fields is often done by women. The crops which the people grow depend on how much water there is.

Millet will grow in dry areas. People can make flour, beer and porridge from millet. In wetter areas, people can grow maize. They may also be able to grow vegetables.

Farmers can irrigate their land near a well or river. On a good farm, there may be plenty of food. They can eat what they need and sell the rest.

In some grassland areas, people live in small family groups. In other places, there are villages and small towns. Today, people often leave their villages. They look for work and more money in the big cities.

Farms and minerals

The cool grasslands, or veld, are in southern Africa. Veld is a Dutch word. It means 'field'. There is high veld and low veld. The high veld is cooler and wetter than the low veld.

▼ These people live in a village in Tanzania. They have harvested their crops. They are now separating the grain from the stalk.

► These people are visiting a national park on the grasslands of Kenya. Without the national parks, some species of animals would have died out. In the parks, animals can live in safety. No one may kill them. People come from all over the world to see the animals.

▼ This is a coal mine in South Africa. You can see how it has been dug out from the flat land around it.

The first European settlers in South Africa were the Dutch. They first went to South Africa over 300 years ago. Later, the British arrived. There was a war between the Dutch and the British. Many Dutch people moved north on a journey called the Great Trek. They settled in the high vèld. Today, there are large farms there. The farmers keep sheep and cattle. They also grow cereal crops.

There are many minerals under the veld. Half the world's gold is mined in South Africa. Other metals mined from the veld are chrome, copper, manganese and uranium. Diamonds and other precious stones are also found there.

Grasslands of southern Asia

The biggest grasslands in southern Asia are in India. Most of them are new grasslands. People have cut down the forests to make farmland.

There are two main areas of grassland in India. On the North Indian Plain, the winters are cool. The summers are hot and wet. The Deccan Plateau runs from north to south, in the centre of India. The Plateau is higher and drier than the Plain. It rains from June to September. This is when the south west **monsoon** winds blow.

▼ These people are planting rice in paddy fields in Thailand. Rice grows best if it is in water for part of the year. Fish can live in the paddy fields. The people can catch and eat them.

▲ These villagers from Bali are threshing rice. They are beating the rice plants against a board. The large round trays are used to separate, or winnow, the grain from the husk.

The farmers

Most farmers in India do not have much land. They can only grow enough food for themselves and their families. They are subsistence farmers.

Many crops grow in India. Wheat is the most important crop in northern India. Cotton is grown on the Deccan Plateau. Farmers on the coast and in the north grow rice. Rice is the main cereal food for many of the people there.

First the farmers plant the rice seeds in small beds. Then, the farmer and his family move the young rice plants to flooded **paddy fields**. The young rice grows well in water. The farmers build low earth walls around the paddy fields. These are called bunds. The bunds keep the water in the fields.

▼ This is one of the oldest ways of getting water from a well on to a field. It is called a Persian wheel.

The rice harvest

A good rice harvest needs rain. If there is not enough rain, the rice crop is poor. The family may go hungry. When there is a good crop, the rice harvest is a busy time. Most people cut the ripe rice by hand. Few farmers can afford machines to help them. Sometimes the farmers group together to buy a machine.

After the rice has been cut, it is **threshed**. Threshing is taking the grains of rice off the stalks. People shake the stalks or beat them against a board.

Then the farmers **winnow** the grain. The rice grains have a tough outer case, or husk. Winnowing means getting rid of the husk. People toss the grains into the air. The husks and rice grains come apart. The lighter husks are blown away by the wind. The heavier rice falls to the ground. Then the rice is dried and stored.

India is the second largest producer of rice after China.

Grasslands of Australasia

Australasia includes Australia, New Zealand, Papua New Guinea and nearby groups of islands. Papua New Guinea is mainly forest. Australia and New Zealand both have large areas of grassland.

Australia has hot, savanna grasslands in the north and cool grasslands in the south. New Zealand has only cool grasslands.

Australian beef farms

Farmers in the grasslands of northern Australia keep beef cattle. It is too dry for any other type of farming. Often, there is only about 4 cm of rain in a year. In some years, it does not rain at all.

There are about 20 million beef cattle in Australia. Some cattle ranches, or stations, are among the largest in the world. The cattle have very large areas to graze on. The farmers only round them up to put the farmers' own mark, or brand, on them, or to take them to market.

Farmers used to drive their cattle overland to the city markets. This meant they had to make the cattle walk. Now good roads link the farming areas with the towns and ports. Huge 'beef trains' made up of cattle trucks travel along these roads. One of the roads is called the Stuart Highway. It is 3000 km long. It runs from Darwin in the north to Adelaide in the south.

◄ This is a 'beef train'. It is carrying large numbers of cattle to the market from a remote cattle station in Australia.

Millions of sheep

There are millions of sheep on the cool grasslands of Australia. There are over 130 million sheep in Australia. The main sheep areas are New South Wales, Queensland, Victoria and Western Australia. Sheep are bred for their wool on the drier pastures. They produce about a quarter of the world's wool. In wetter areas, sheep are bred for their meat.

An important job in sheep farming is shearing. This is taking the wool off a sheep. There are large sheep shearing gangs. They travel from farm to farm.

Farming in New Zealand

New Zealand has more rain than Australia. It was once mainly forest. People cut down the trees to make grasslands which are very fertile. Farmers keep cattle for their meat and milk. They also keep large flocks of sheep for meat and wool.

▲ These sheep are on South Island, New Zealand. Many of the sheep farms are close to the ports. The meat and wool are exported around the world.

▼ Sheep shearing is a skilled job. In 1976, one person sheared a record 353 lambs in a nine-hour day.

Grasslands in danger

The grasslands of the world are changing. In many countries, farmers want to use the natural grasslands. People need more food. New farming methods mean crops can be grown in dry areas. The natural grasses may die out.

▼ Settlers on the Great Plains in the United States ploughed up the land to grow wheat. In the 1930s, there were several years of drought. There was no grass left to bind the soil. Strong winds blew the soil away. A dust bowl was made where there was once natural grassland. Much of the land has now been reclaimed.

There are other dangers to the grasslands. Cities are growing larger. They spread into the countryside. Houses, factories, roads and railways are built on the grasslands.

Plants and animals

Wildlife can suffer when people start to farm the land. People destroy wild plants. They chop down trees. They plant crops instead of wild grasses. They spray chemicals on to crops. They burn the grasslands. Wild plants become rare.

Animals suffer when we destroy the plants. Many animals depend on the wild plants for food. Insects need the leaves and flowers. Insects die from lack of food without these. Farmers also use chemicals to protect their crops from insects. Without insects, other animals may suffer. Many birds need insects for food. Both

The Dust Bowl

birds and small animals can also die in grassland fires.

Larger grassland animals are now in danger. People have taken over their land. Many have been killed or moved away from the grasslands. Today, many of the large grassland animals survive only in special parks. There are national parks in many countries where wild animals are protected by laws.

Making deserts

Grass roots hold water. The water helps to bind the soil together. When animals eat too much of the grass, the soil becomes bare. There are not enough roots to hold water and bind the soil. When this happens, rain can wash the soil away. The wind can also blow the soil away. This is called **erosion**.

Erosion can also happen if people grow one crop on the same land for a long time. The soil loses its goodness. It turns into a dry powder. This happened in the United States in the 1930s. For several years there were very strong winds in the spring. They carried away large amounts of soil. Once the soil was gone, a desert was left behind. It was called the Dust Bowl. It covered a large part of Texas, Oklahoma, Kansas and Colorado. Farmers have been able to make some of this land fertile again. A lot of it is still useless land.

Soil erosion is a big problem in many countries. In Africa today, the Sahara Desert is getting larger every year. There are more farms on the African savanna. There is less room for the cattle herders. The herders cannot find fresh grass for their animals. The cattle stay too long in one place and destroy the grass. The land turns to desert.

Grasslands of the future

We need to protect the grasslands. If they disappear, the wildlife that live on the grasslands will disappear too. We also need to protect the forests. Each year, large areas are cut down to make farmland.

Trees hold large amounts of water. When the sun shines, moisture rises into the air. Later, it turns back into water and falls as rain. If we chop down large areas of forest, we stop this happening. There would be less rain and fewer crops could be grown.

New grasslands

We need to find new ways of making land to farm. Then, we would not need to use so much grassland or forest.

One way to do this is to farm the deserts. We can find water by drilling deep wells. Then, we can water the desert. People have irrigated many desert lands. People can grow fruit and vegetables in parts of the desert areas in the Middle East.

Another way to make farmland is to drain marshes. Salt marshes lie close to the sea. The land is wet and salty. It can be made into farmland. In the Netherlands, people have drained land that was once under the sea. Reeds are then planted. The reeds bind the mud to make soil. Later, other plants will grow. Land of this kind is called a **polder**. The polders of the Netherlands make good grazing land for dairy cattle.

▼ These sheep are grazing on a polder in the Netherlands. The land used to be under the sea.

Grasslands for people

Parks and gardens are small areas of grassland made by people. They are important places in and around our crowded cities. People can enjoy walking and playing in them. Some parks are more like the countryside. Wild plants and animals live there. We could make more parks in our towns and cities.

We have harmed much of the land near our cities. There are great heaps of earth and rock left from mining. There are wastelands where factories used to be. We can make these places into grassland again. We can plant grass. Other plants and flowers will soon appear. Birds and insects will follow. Small animals will make their homes in the grass.

If we are careful, we can make room for many living things in our cities. We do not need to take all the land ourselves in the future.

▲ People have learned how to grow crops in the desert. The green circles in the distance are fields which have been irrigated so wheat can be grown.

▼ The Liverpool Garden Festival was held in 1984 and 1985. Much of the land here was once wasteland. Now, it is being used again.

Glossary

acacia: the name of a group of small trees and shrubs found in warm countries

adapt: to change in order to suit different surroundings

agriculture: the cultivation or use of the soil to grow crops

alfalfa: a type of grass planted by farmers for their cattle. It is also known as lucerne

annual: something that happens once a year. A plant that lives for only one year

bark: the outer layer of a tree trunk or branch

bird of prey: a bird that kills and eats other animals. Birds of prey include eagles, hawks and buzzards

browser: an animal which wanders from plant to plant eating the leaves, stems or twigs

burrow: the underground home of an animal. Animals dig burrows for defence and shelter

camouflage: the colour pattern or body shape which help to hide an animal's body in its surroundings

campos: the tropical grasslands of central South America

caravan: a group of people and their animals travelling across the desert

cash crop: a crop which people grow to sell rather than use themselves

cereal: a kind of grass whose seeds we eat. Wheat, maize and rice are all cereals

chemical: any substance which can change when joined to or mixed with another substance. Some chemicals are used to protect crops

climate: the usual weather conditions of a region or country, throughout the year. The climate differs from one area to another

collective: of a group. A kind of farm in the USSR run by a group of people

combine harvester: a machine used in harvesting crops

conquer: to defeat an enemy

conservation: the protection and careful use of the countryside, wildlife and other natural resources

continent: a large piece of land sometimes including many countries. The Earth is divided into seven continents

crops: the plants grown to produce food. Wheat and maize are crops

cultivate: to use land to grow crops

domesticate: to tame. Domestic animals are kept by people and are no longer wild

downs: grassy fields. The cool grasslands of Australia and New Zealand are called downs

drought: a long time without rain

empire: several countries or groups of people all ruled by one person or group of people

Equator: the imaginary circle which goes around the centre of the Earth. The Equator divides the northern part of the Earth from the southern part. The hottest parts of the world are near the Equator

erosion: the wearing away of the land by water, ice or the wind. The wind erodes the land by blowing away the soil

export: goods sent to another country to be sold. Beef is an export from Argentina

factory: a building where goods are made

fertile: describes rich soil where seeds and plants can grow well

food chain: a chain or series of living things which depend on each other for food. A typical food chain starts with a plant which is eaten by a plant-eating animal. The plant-eating animal is then eaten by a meat-eating animal

fuel: material which burns. Fuel burned in engines makes power for movement

government: a group of people who control a country through laws and rules

grain: the seeds of the grasses which we grow as cereals

grassland: a large area of land which is too dry for trees to grow

graze: to feed on grass. Sheep and cattle are grazing animals

grazer: an animal which feeds on grass

habitat: the place where an animal usually lives

harvest: the time when crops are gathered in. The crops themselves

herder: a person who keeps a flock or herd of cattle, sheep or goats

industry: the work to do with the making or producing of goods

invent: to make something new

irrigation: a way of bringing water by pipe or river to land which has little rain. The water is pumped from rivers, lakes or from under the ground. Irrigation makes it possible to grow crops in dry places

llanos: the tropical grasslands of the northern part of South America

lucerne: a type of grass planted by farmers for their cattle. It is also known as alfalfa

machine: something that uses power or energy to do work. Machines such as tractors help farmers to do their work more easily

meadow: a field of grass which is often cut for hay

migration: the movement of animals from one area to another. Animals migrate long distances to find food, to produce young, or to escape from cold weather. These long journeys happen at certain times each year

mineral: any natural substance found in the ground which has not been formed from plant or animal life. Rocks and metals are minerals

monsoon: a strong wind that changes direction according to the season. Monsoons bring heavy rain to South East Asia in the summer

natural: something that exists in the world around us. Natural grasslands grow without people planting them

natural resource: something useful the exists in the world around us, but is not made by people. Oil and minerals are natural resources

nomad: someone who moves from place to place in search of food or to find food for animals

ore: any rock from which metal can be taken

paddy field: a field used for growing rice

pampas: the cool grasslands of South America. They cover parts of Argentina, Brazil and Uruguay

pastoral: to do with grazing animals like sheep or cattle. People who travel from place to place looking for fresh grass for their animals are called pastoral nomads

pasture: a piece of land covered in grass where animals feed

perennial: lasting through the year. A plant that lives for more than two years

plain: a large, open area of flat land. Plains are usually covered in grass

plateau: a large area of high flat land

polder: a Dutch word for land that was once under the sea

population: the total number of people living in a country or one place

prairie: a large, open area of grassland without trees. The grasslands of North America are called prairies

predator: an animal which lives by hunting and eating other animals

prey: an animal which is hunted and eaten by other animals

rain forest: a type of forest that grows in the tropics where it is hot and wet

rain shadow: an area of little rain on the side of a mountain furthest from the sea

ranch: a large farm for sheep or cattle

reclaim: to make waste land useful again

refinery: a place where the raw crude oil from the ground is made pure. Petrol, diesel oil and other products are made at refineries

rodent: a member of a group of small animals with long, sharp front teeth which are used for gnawing. Mice, rats and squirrels are rodents

savanna: a hot, dry grassland with few trees. The hot grasslands of Africa are called the savanna

scavenger: an animal which feeds on waste food or on the remains of food left by other animals. Scavengers also feed on dead animals

season: one of the four periods of time during the year. The seasons are Spring, Summer, Autumn and Winter. Each season has a certain type of weather

settle: to stay in one place in order to make a home

shrub: a low plant with woody stalks with branches near the ground. Shrubs do not have single trunks like trees

species: a group of animals or plants which look alike and can breed with one another. It takes two adults of the same species to produce young

staple: the main type of food that someone eats. Millet is the staple food in parts of Africa

state: a country or a part of a country. In the USSR, a state farm is one that is owned by the government

steppe: a kind of dry grassland. The grasslands of eastern Europe and Asia are called the steppes

subsistence: a kind of farming. A subsistence farmer usually grows just enough food to keep himself and his family alive, and has nothing left over to sell

survive: to stay alive

swarm: a large group of bees, ants or locusts. They gather together to move to a new nest or feeding ground

temperate: describes a climate which has mild summers and cool winters. The weather is never very hot or very cold

termite: a type of insect, like an ant, which lives in large groups, or colonies

thresh: to beat crops, such as wheat or rice, in order to make the grain fall off the stalks

traditional: describes something that has been handed down from parents to their children for many years

tree line: the upper limit above which trees will not grow

tropical: describes something to do with, or coming from, the tropics. The tropics are the very hot, damp regions of the Earth found on either side of the Equator. The Tropic of Cancer marks the most northern line of the tropics and the Tropic of Capricorn marks the most southern line

veld: the cool grasslands of southern Africa

winnow: to get rid of the tough part from the outside of grain

Index